COLOR TEST PAGE

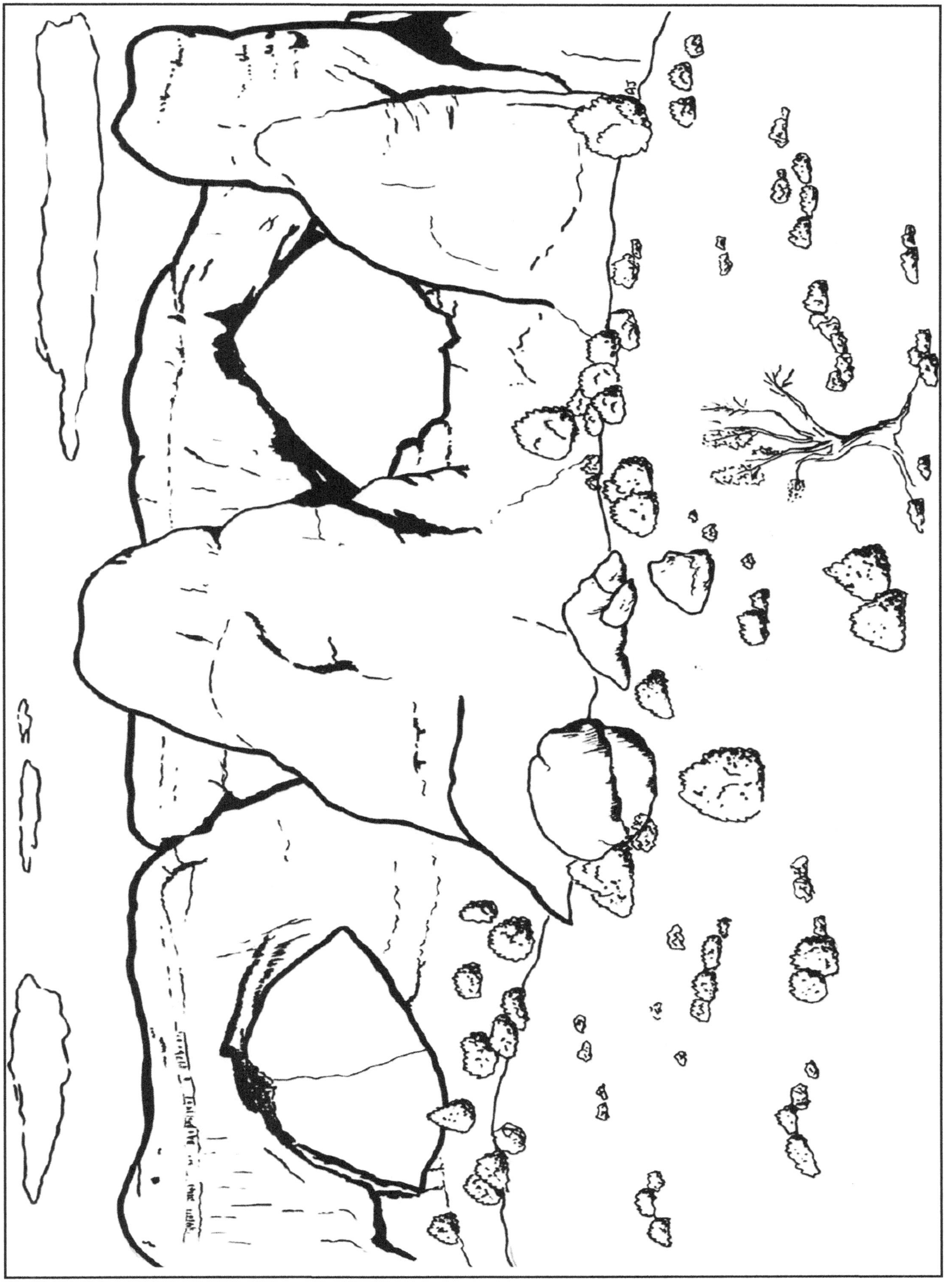

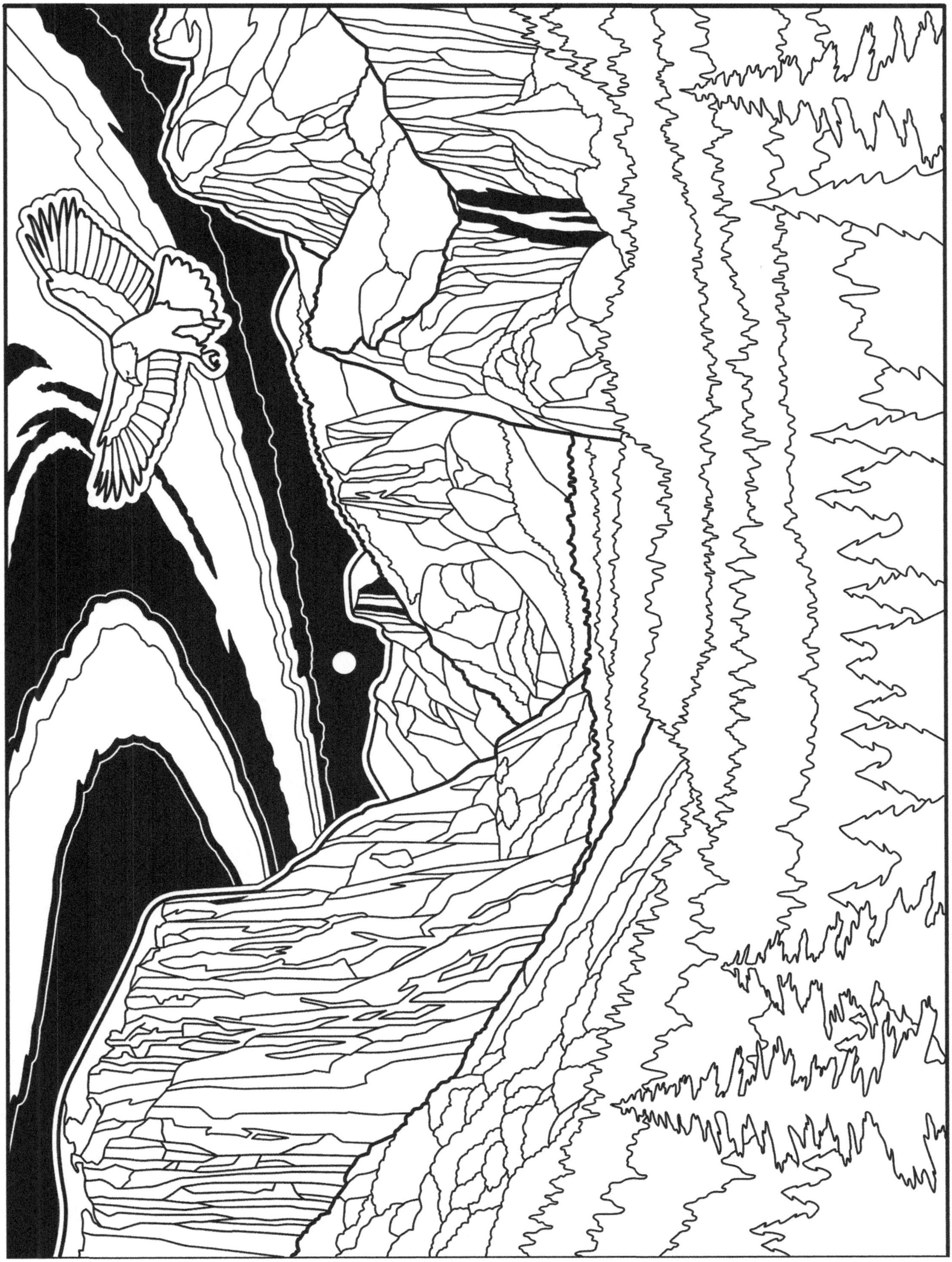

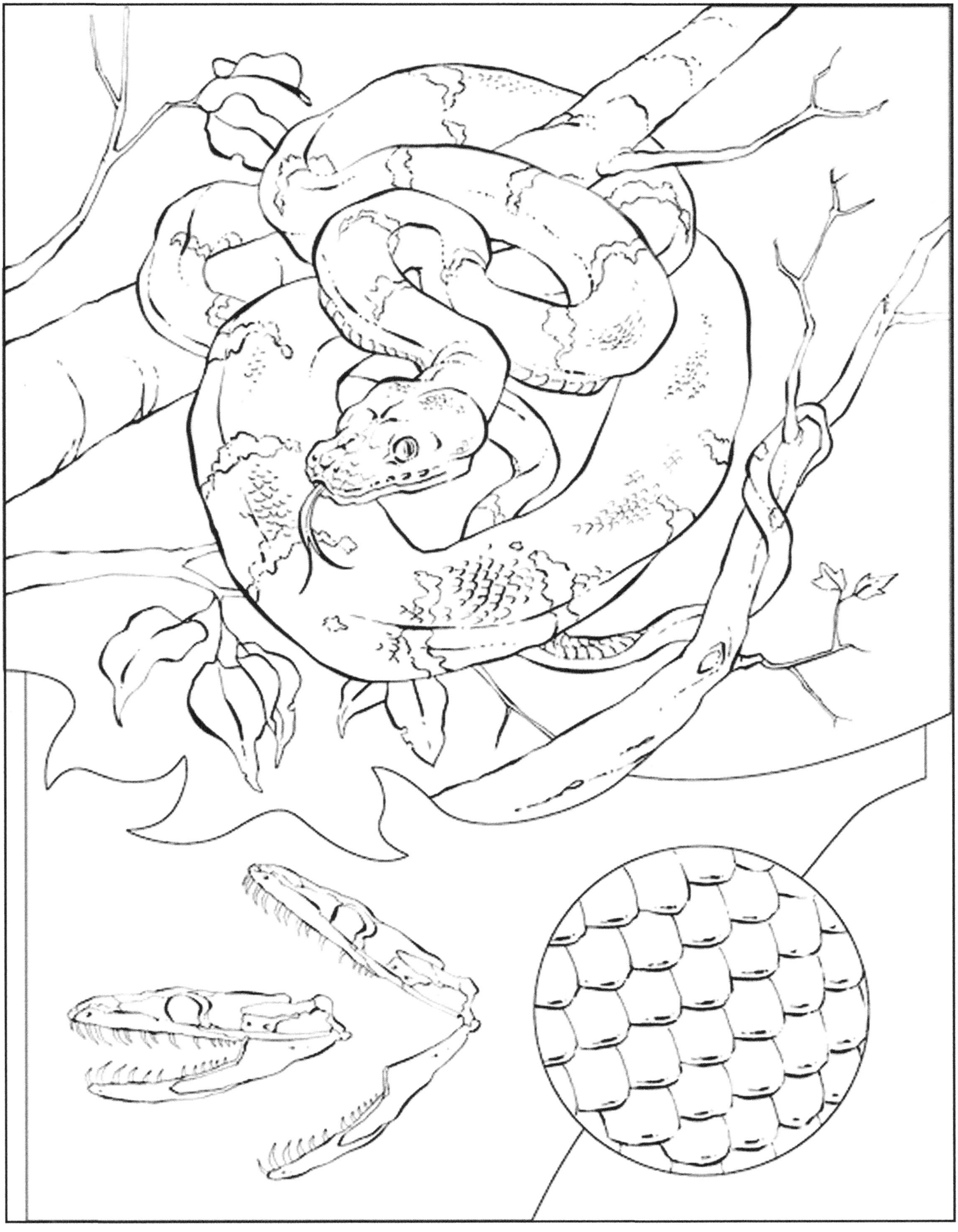

Ranger Station 1
Ranger Station 2

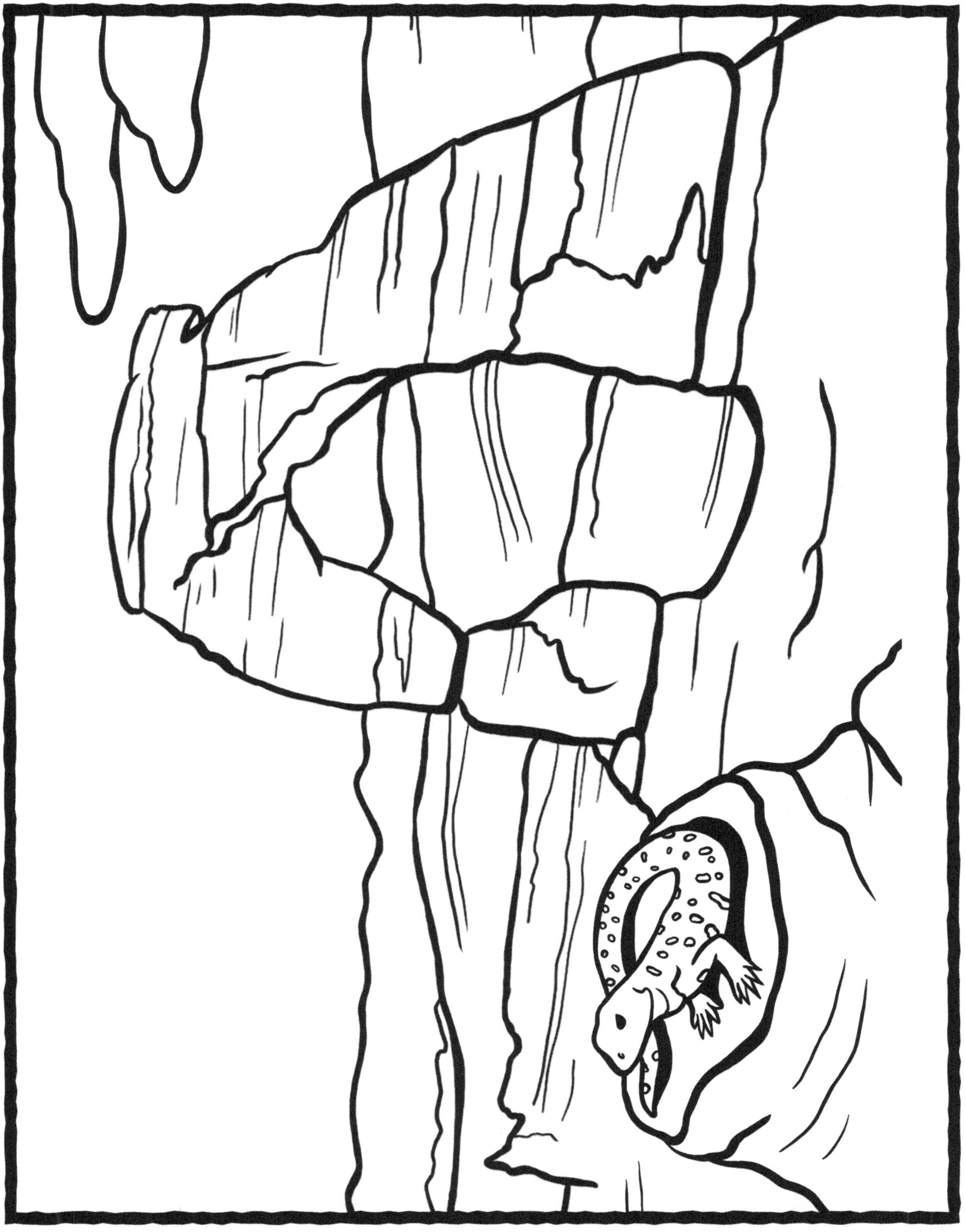

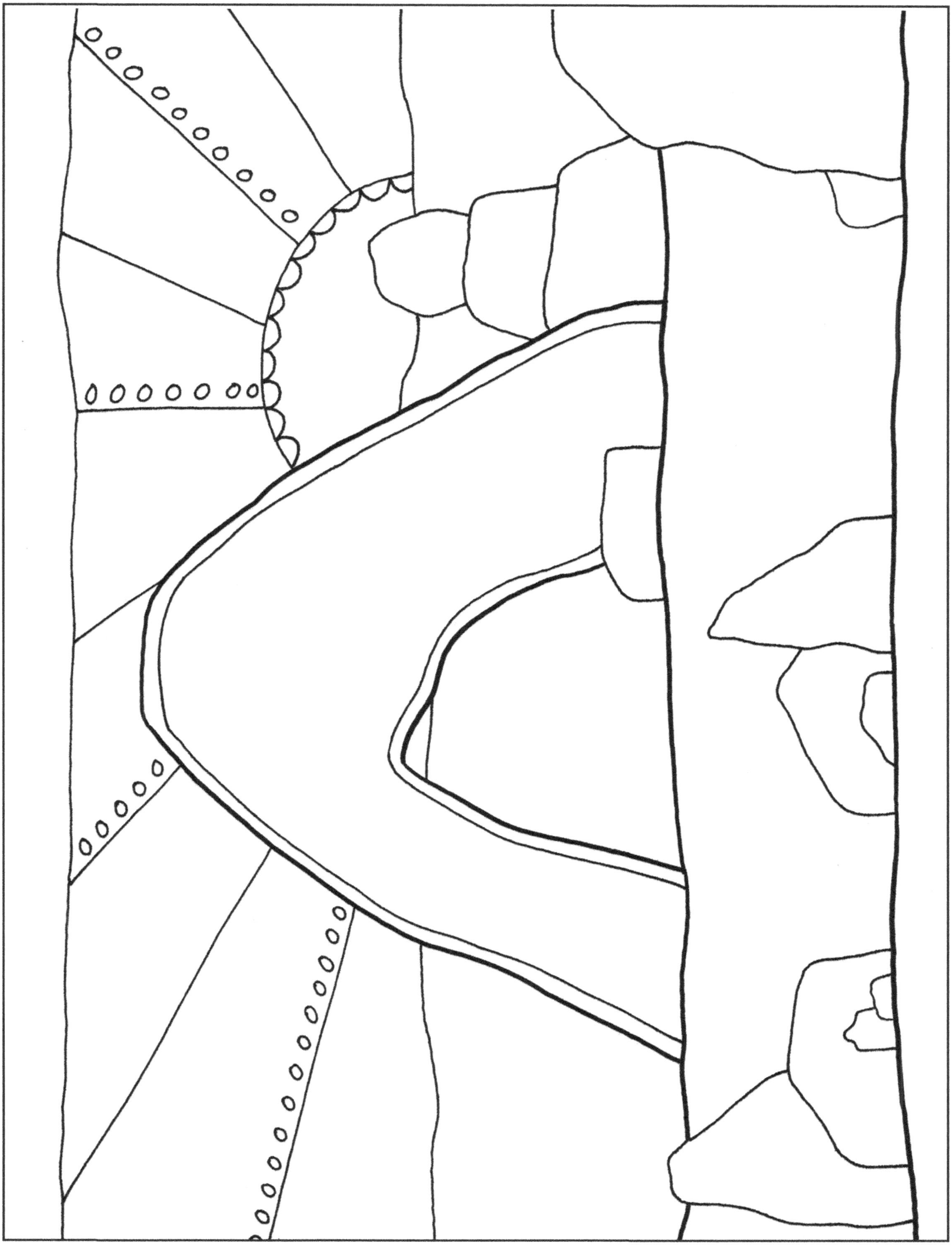

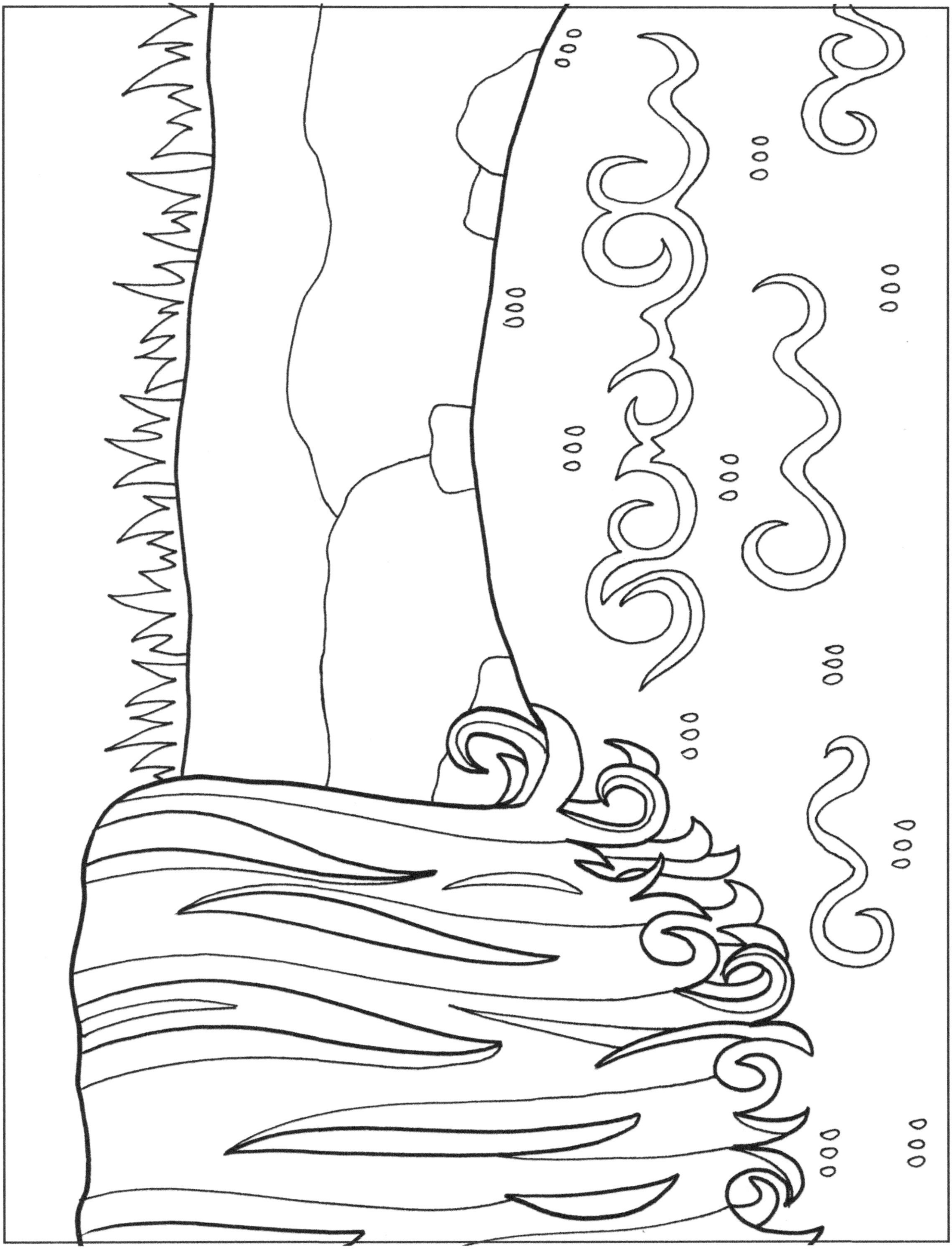

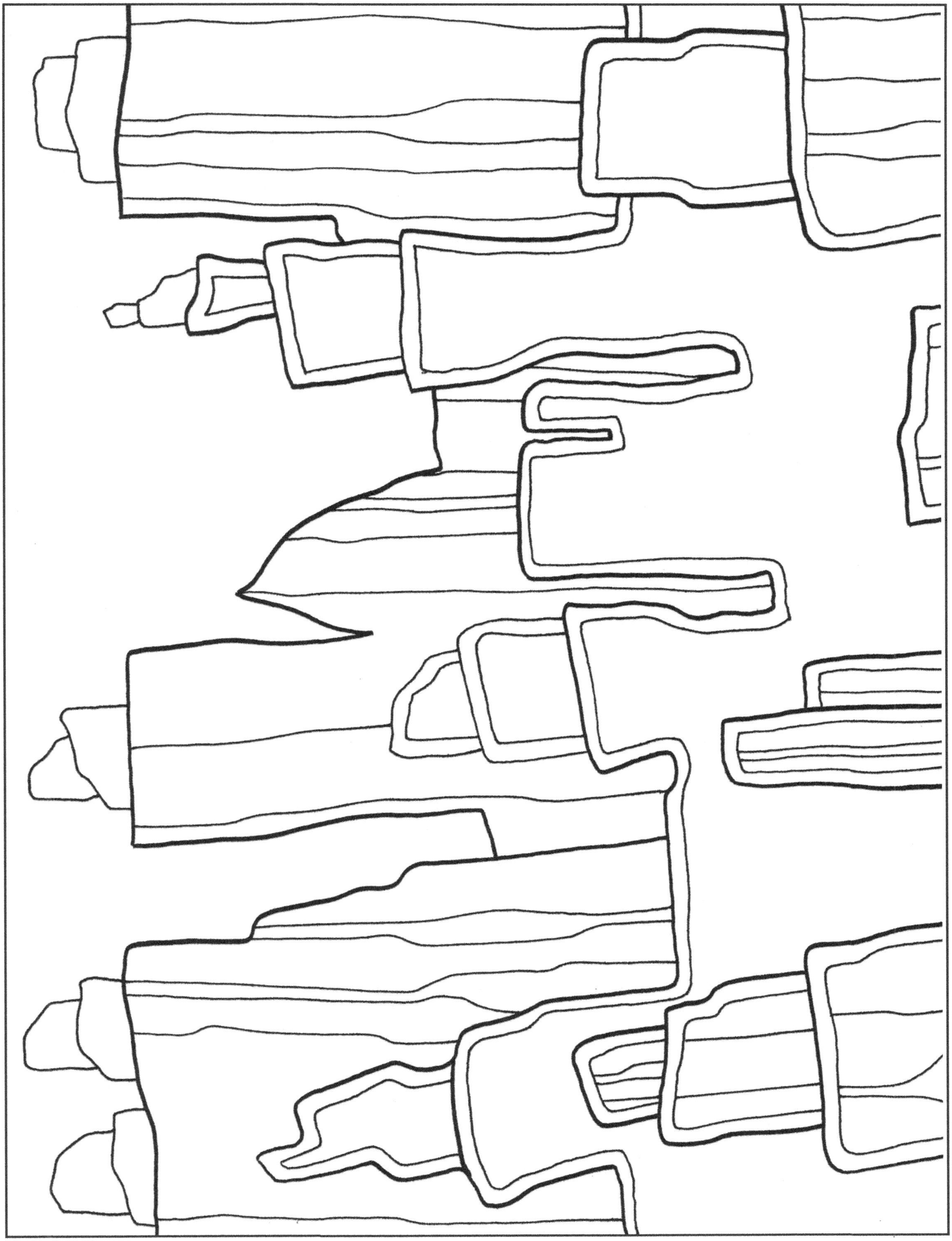